PRAGMATISM BROUGHT UPFRONT

P

P

CONTENTS

<u>AN UNFULIFILLED WISH</u>

INTRODUCTION

I just completed writing the last paper of my 6th Semester examination. As I exited the examination hall, the feeling of relief was written over everyone's face as it was the end of another enthralling semester as I along with a bunch of my friends headed towards to the nearest Dominos to celebrate the end of the semester. I was quietly confident about my performance in the examination and was in anticipation of my results. The discussion soon turned towards the topic of placements many of my friends were to join many top MNC's as interns most of them wanted their internships to be converted to Pre-Placement offers as they wanted to escape the tensions of a gruelling placement season.

I thought to myself this is likely to be a thrill a minute ride like the one I have never experienced before. I headed back home with hope and anxiety of what was to come.

My phone was constantly buzzing with mails about placement preparation tests and tips I chose to ignore them for now as I was keener on enjoying my summer vacation.

The First Pre-Placement Talk:

A preplacement talk was scheduled during the second week of our summer vacation. It was a talk which explained to us about the placement policy of the institute and the etiquettes that one needs to follow in an interview. The Dean of our institute was to address the gathering. He went on to explain about the rich history of the institute and its placement statistics. Thus, preparing us for what was to come. The general message from the pre-placement talk was to be confident and not try and lose hope.

Impact of the talk

he pre-placement talk had a prominent impact on my mind. This was when I suddenly realised that I had to start preparing for my placements, but I did not know from where to start. I was albeit very confused and could not focus on a single topic as we had studied a wide variety of subjects during our previous semesters.

There were a number of preplacement seminars which were organised by the institute in order to help us get acquainted with the process of placements these were of some help as it helped us gain confidence

I was quietly confident about my preparation, I was about to attend my first placement test the next morning, It was a tough night to sleep thoughts gushed into my head. I rehearsed the interview many times in my own mind. That morning when I first entered the hall I was a bit nervous. I took up a seat in the middle rows. The placement coordinator welcomed us into the hall and wished us well for our placement season. He explained the rules pertaining to the placement season. The HR of the company arrived and explained about the job profile, and the events that were planned for the day. I was pretty nervous as I entered the lab where the tests were being conducted I sat down in from of the system and the test began the test went smoothly I was quietly confident about the test. Soon the results of the first round was announced. I could not make it through to the next round. I was disappointed but was still confident about my chances in the coming days.

Classes begin

Our 7th semester classes began and most of us were not too keen on attending classes as we were more worried about placements. There was cheer in the class among those who were placed. There was fear and apprehension amongst many in the class about what was in store for them. Days turned into weeks but I unfortunately could not get through the first round. This was when self-doubt started creeping through my mind. Retaining focus was key to success this was when my peer group helped me a lot. This was when all the bonding that we had over the years came into the foreground where each one of us worked hand in hand for collective success. Success was equally well celebrated. My apprehensions refused to die down with each passing day the anxiety of not being placed was increasing. Due to a lovely support system created to us by our institute we had to look nowhere else for help. Will all the support systems and my lovely peer group help me succeed. Is a story for another day? There was a wonderful person in my peer group who was a person who hated losing and always wanted to be on the top of the tree We dwell about his experiences in the next part.

CHAPTER 2
AIM FOR THE STARS

He was the person that everyone is envious about everyone wanted to emulate him. He was considered to be the best amongst equals. His set his sights far beyond our reach. Everyone was always curious to know as to what he does to

Stay on top of the tree. As people say successful men never share their secret he never did. However, there was one occasion where I feel that I got a sneak-peek into his mind.

It was on the day before the entire placement process was to begin. I was at his place preparing for the gruelling season ahead of me. This was when he exclaimed that He was aiming to get an admission into the world's top university for his higher education. He was considered to be a notch above the rest. So it was natural for him to aim for the moon while we aimed at the tree. I asked him if he ever felt like he was under pressure to perform as everyone expected him to do really well He replied to this statement by stating that he looked at situations differently, thus enabling him to aim higher. This was like a cryptic message which I tried to decipher but failed. When placements did begin he was placed in a top multinational company on Day 2. This achievement would have made everyone proud. His sights were set higher he was happy but not entirely satisfied with his efforts. He put his blood and sweat to prepare for the all-important examination which would enable him to fulfil his dream of being a student in the world's topmost university.

It was the day of the result. Did he succeed in making his dream come true is a story in itself? Being a dunce is a very hard thing to do just like being on top of the tree both demand you to be consistent in your effort. The next part of the story deals with one such a person who was a part of our group.

CHAPTER 3
A DIFFERENT PERSONA

He was one guy who rarely cared to sit through the rigours of classes. He was one guy who rarely cared about anything in life. We all wondered if he ever felt any pressure, he spent most of his time outside the class than inside it. However, he was the person whom you would consider to be street-smart. He was a wonderful man manager, He stood first when it came to managing events at college.

When placements actually began as all of us were nervous. He remained his usual self. Seldom worrying about what was to come. This very peculiar behaviour made us wonder as to when this guy would take life a bit-more seriously.

He would choose his preferences carefully and would spend more time looking at the company's profile more than anyone of us would. Does this mean that he had a very clear idea as to what he wanted to do in his career? A clarity of thought we all struggled to have at this point in our lives.

We have looked at 3 distinct and unique individuals in these stories. The question now that haunts us is who was right with their thought processes. Will all of them succeed?

CHAPTER 4
ONE BAD DECISION

The first question was did I ever succeed in clearing the first round? In the meantime the results of the examination which guaranteed our topper a seat in the university of his dreams was out. He had missed out by a whisker, This was probably the first time in my life that I had seen a guy being so dejected in his life. The once cheerful and happy soul now was a shadow of its past he refused take part in celebrations and started losing interest in life. Everything that once seemed happy now looked sad. We were worried about him but since he was an introvert by nature. Too much needling would cause distress. Will this guy ever be back to his normal self we all wondered. He was a guy who needed help but would not seek it. Thus making it harder for himself and the rest around him The system that we were all proud of had failed us and something had to be done really quickly to prevent a precious life from being lost. Unfortunately, nothing could be done as the guy whom we all adored had jumped off the roof of his house and lost his dear life.

Were his desires responsible for his death? Did the System fail him? Was he not the person whom he seemed to be? These are a few questions to which answers needed to be found. Irrespective of whether the answers are found or not. We all lost a friend who can never be replaced.

The next question that needs an answer to is the guy who was considered a dunce. Did he ever succeed? Did he ever become serious in his life? The answer to this question is a big YES. Like it was known previously he was one guy who was keen on doing only the things he wanted to do. This quality of the person made him stand-out amongst the rest. He eventually did succeed but not the way we all imagined.

As each us were busy preparing for interviews. He went on to solve a problem. Which made him gain immediate recognition. Since he was a person who liked to remain outside the class more often than not he had a very keen eye on the various problems of the real world which we would have no time for. One such a problem was to enable people without smartphones to access services which were provided by various governments and other organizations. His solved this problem by developing an EPBAX system which provided a centralised toll-free number which enabled the end user to gain access to services through an IVRS based system, this effort of his was widely appreciated and he received a number of awards and accolades for the same. He even raised funding to start his company on a commercial scale.

This again goes on to show that a person who wandered around aimlessly and showed no desire to succeed actually succeeded. Thus bringing us back to the same question as to
Whether our desires are responsible for our doom? Do we need to take life as it comes instead of chasing something that we may never get?

The answer to the question that all of you were waiting for "Yes, I did clear a job interview" but decided to join the dunce in his effort to make this world a better place. Make sure you guys give those questions a deep thought. Until next time Goodbye.

* * *

THE LAST LUNCH

CHAPTER 1
RUN FOR COVER

I vividly remember that day, the sun was shining bright as we all were at the table waiting for lunch to be served. Little girl Anna had just completed her drawing. It was the picture of a happy family picture with five people. Me, my elder brother mother, father and little Anna. Mommy was busy preparing lunch. Father had just completed the work in the garden. Elder brother had just completed his football game and had returned home.

There was tension all around the country there was the threat of a war. There were many demonstrations held in the major cities of the country. However, since we lived on the country side our lives were impacted to a lesser extent. Just as we completed our lunch and dad was above to take a nap we heard the roaring sounds of jets flying over our heads. The noise was loud but what was to follow would change our lives forever. We suddenly heard a deafening sound windows pane broke and the earth shook. We were all in shock and did not know how to react. We saw people running helter-skelter through a broken window. Father had got hit on the head by a wooden plank which fell off the roof he was bleeding. Little Anna was frightened and hid behind a wall. I and my elder brother escaped unhurt.

Just as we were trying to come to terms with what was happening we heard another explosion but this time it had struck closer. We ventured out of the house to see the barn on fire we rushed out with buckets and tried to douse the flames as jets blazed over our head. We were all scared suddenly there was smoke billowing out of houses. Life had turned upside down. We decided to leave our house and head to safety. Ambulances were busy shifting the injured to the hospital as we tried to pack whatever we could find and left. It got hold of Anna's drawing and put it into my backpack. We climbed on to our Minivan and headed out of town. Roads were badly damaged due to the bombing thus making it hard to drive as we saw rubble all around and raging infernos with wailing cries of people awaiting help. As we headed out of town we heard from a local Radio station that all of this was the result of an air-raid. It was then we realised that we were at war.

As we headed out of the town towards the city there were many camps which setup for were the displaced. We checked into one of those camps and we suddenly were left homeless. Food was served in the camp. As the night set in there were apprehensions about another air raid as midnight approached the city was bombed again this time the car park next to the camp was destroyed injuring scores of people. We lost our minivan. We were now left without a vehicle to escape in the case of danger. Little was known about what happened to our house back in the village

The next morning the President addressed the nation as we listened to a radio station in the camp. He said "The nation is under attack we shall not bow down to the strength of the enemy but fight back with all our might" as he concluded his address there were more bombings that took place. This was when father realised that it was not safe for them to stay here anymore. He asked mother and Anna to board a flight to a neighbouring country and he said the rest of the family would join them whenever possible as he had just enough cash to book two tickets. ATM's were non-functional and electronic transactions could not be completed due to the communication system breaking down.

We headed to the airport in a taxi. As we entered the airport we headed towards the counter and asked for the next fight to the neighbouring country. We booked our tickets Anna and Mommy boarded the flight. Just as we returned to the camp. We heard an announcement on a local radio station about a civilian plane being shot down mistakenly for a military aircraft. Little was known about the plane and its passengers.

Were Anna and Mommy passengers of that flight? Did they reach their destination?

CHAPTER 2
THE UNEXPECTED SEPERATION

We were all very anxious and worried as we headed to the airport. We unfortunately did not get much information at the airport. We feared for the worst but kept hoping against hope that nothing would go wrong. Just as we sat down the chairs in the lobby. We heard the announcement that the nation's airspace was declared a no-fly zone and all flights stand cancelled. Just when the announcement was completed we heard the sound of gunfire, the airport was under attack and we were under siege. We all ran in different directions to save our dear lives I ran towards the exit and managed to get out of the airport but I did not find Daddy or my elder brother again. I tried to fanatically search for them but soon the airport was under lockdown and thus little could be done. I waited for the siege to end it was a terrible feeling. I always felt that there could be nothing worse than this that could happen to anyone.

After 3 long days of gun battle the siege was over as the gunmen who had been holed up had been eliminated. As I went into the airport looking for my father and elder brother, I feared for the worst and my heart kept skipping a beat whenever is saw a corpse. Cries and screams of people echoed across the hall. I could not see my brother or my father after a thorough search I decided to enlist their names amongst the missing suddenly I was all alone. I wished and prayed that they would be safe.

I returned to the camp and was waiting for news about my brother and father. Little was known about Anna and Mommy too. As I sat in despair I overheard a group of people speaking about a plan to flee the country by crossing the border in the hope of better prospects. I thought for a while and realised that it would not be safe to stay in the camp for a long time. I went up to them and asked them if I could join them in their plan to leave the country. They viewed me with a suspicion at first but an elderly man who was present in that group convinced the others in the group to take me along with them.

The plan was that the next day morning we would all take the rail to the last town of the land and from there we would cross over the border. This was a dangerous journey as we all had the fear of being caught by the border guards on both sides of the border and we had to swim across a river to reach the other side.

The next morning, we all walked our way to the railway station I had no money to buy a ticket. So I thought that I cannot make it out of the country. This was when the old man bought me a ticket with the last penny in his pocket. This was when I decided that the old man was a part of my family now and decided to never let go of him.

It was a 3-hour journey. There was widespread damage and destruction along the course of the journey. We reached our destination and disembarked from the train. We had not eaten since the previous night but I had no money to buy anything. We were about 5-kilometers from the border. We walked our way up the hill to reach a border post. Since it was wartime all the troops were on high alert and it was practically impossible to get past them without being shot. It was afternoon and the sun was blazing above our heads exhaustion was creeping in we decided to split up into groups of two and wait for nightfall to execute our plans.
At the dead of night, we attempted to cross over barbed wire. The alarms went off and the guards opened fire we ran for our lives many people in our group unfortunately could not make it. The old man was hit by a bullet on his leg this left him immobilised. I did not want to let go but he looked into my eyes and said "Dear boy please go may God be with you" I tried to convince him but he persuaded me to cross the border. I let him go with a heavy heart. As the sound of gun-fire was ringing in my ear I managed to cross over the border.

At the other side of the border, we took cover from the incoming fire. Our troubles were far from over we had to swim across a raging river to reach safety. I was adept at swimming thanks to all the training that was given by my Dad. He jumped into the river the current was fast but managed to swim across and make it to safety. A total of five people managed to make it to safety.

The next challenge was to seek refuge and look for a work to lead my livelihood. We five people moved in towards a border-post where we indicated surrender. We were arrested by the military. As I was taken into custody there were many questions that lingered in my mind.

What happened to my Mother and Anna? Where are my brother and father? What is my life now? The good news was that I had a roof over my head and could sleep peacefully without the fear of being bombed. Will I ever find answers to all my questions?

CHAPTER 3
A NEW LIFE WITH OLD SCARS

We were taken to a camp where we were housed for the next day. Unsure of what to expect I sat down thinking about my family. I was anxious and wanted to know if they were safe but did not know how. We were all taken to a court where we were remanded to police custody.

The police interrogated us about our intentions. The conditions inside prison were harsh we feared for our lives gang wars were frequent inside the prison. We feared that we would have to spend the rest of our lives inside the walls of a prison in an unknown country. We prayed that we be released and allowed to rebuild our livelihoods.

Our prayers were soon answered we were all released without any charges. The ordeal however was not over as we had to apply for an asylum to seek work in that country. It was due to the efforts of a human rights activist that we were able to apply for an asylum. While our asylum was still under process. I began to do odd jobs for a living. It was barely enough and I often ate a single meal a day. I was however determined not to give up hope and also wanted to reunite with my family.

Days passed our asylum was still under process but the war in my homeland was over. I wanted to return back home but was unsure as there was large scale devastation and poverty. I decided to stay back in this foreign land in the hope for a better future. At the back of my mind however I always had the intentions of returning back home and look for my family without whom I would be incomplete.

Our applications for asylum were soon processed. I was granted residency for a period of one year. This status enabled me to complete my college degree. I soon enrolled myself in the Bachelor of Science program at a famous university in the capital. The university was gracious enough to provide me a complete fee waiver.

With great aspirations and hope I started attending my college. While I attended college I made good friends, there was no discrimination on the campus. Everything seemed to be going well. Six months into college I wrote my first semester examination. The results were out, I had done well. I was happy with my results.

Soon my second semester began it was the first day of classes. The Principal of the college came into our classroom and introduced us to a new professor who had joined the college recently. As the principal introduced the new professor to the class I was in for a pleasant surprise the professor was none other than Mr Smith our neighbour back home. After the class was over I went over to Mr Smith and introduced myself. He instantly recognised and took me home. He had moved in to this country with his family when the war broke out. Mr Smith and his wife insisted that I stay with them at their place. They also promised me that they would help me locate and reunite with my family

I gained more confidence and hope that with Mr Smith's assistance I would be able to reunite with my family. The road ahead was a bumpy one full of thorns. What exactly had happened to my parents, brother and little Anna?

CHAPTER 4
THE SEARCH BEGINS

The search for my parents began when on a weekend we went back to our homeland. It was the first time since the war had ended that I set foot on that land our home was in ruins and the place was strewn with debris. It was none like the place we called home. As I walked across our farm I found a small necklace with a small emerald pendent attached to it the stone gleamed in the shining sun.

I recalled that it was my mother's favourite jewel. Dad had presented her the necklace on her birthday last year. As tears swelled up my eyes I prayed for my family. We soon left the place, Mr Smith comforted me by saying "We will find your family don't worry everything will be fine"

We then went to the police station to file a missing complaint. We were asked to prove our identity before we could do so however, I did not have any document to prove that I was my father's son and that we were citizens of this country. We tried to explain our position to the officer but he said that he was helpless in the matter as he had to follow rules.

I felt utterly dejected and could not hold back my tears. We returned back to our adopted home. I was soon consoled by Mr Smith's family. They asked me not to lose hope and said that they would leave no stone unturned in finding my family. I thanked them profusely for their love care and support. I was more determined to find out about my loved ones and bring about a closure to the case.

We were however, unsure of the path that we had to follow in the quest for finding my family. The following week we went back to the school where I studied and requested for a copy of my school certificates as it will help me prove my identity. The school authorities said that the war had destroyed all infrastructure and all the records had been gutted in a fire caused by a bombing. The principal expressed his inability to help. We then realised that this was going to be tougher than what we previously thought. We refused to give up hope and went back to our adopted land.

One day as I looked at the necklace that I found in the farm and was recalling all the memories related to it. An idea struck me that we could get a DNA test done from the very tiny strands of hair follicles that were stuck to the necklace this would form an undeniable proof that I was the son of my parents and thus the police would believe in our story

I went and informed about my idea to Mr Smith, He welcomed my idea and said that he would provide all the necessary assistance in getting the DNA test done. The following week we went to a government accredited laboratory and explained our problem to them. They said that it was illegal for them to perform a DNA test unless authorised by a court of law.

We then went back to our homeland and met a lawyer and explained him about our case. He said that he would help us get justice. We soon filed a petition before a court of law to allow us to get a DNA test conducted that would help me prove my identity and help in resolving the case. The court ruled in our favour and asked us to get the DNA profiling test. We were overjoyed. The results the DNA tests were out. I was able to prove that I was the son of my parents and thus proving my citizenship. It was a small victory.

We lodged a missing complaint on the basis of the DNA test report the police said that they would assist me in every way possible to help me reunite with my family.

CHAPTER 5
THE INVESTIGATION BEGINS

The police began their investigations into the case. They verified facts about my mother and little Anna boarding the flight on that ill-fated day. It was soon established that they had indeed boarded the flight.

Investigations revealed that the plane had suffered a crash and not hit by a missile as thought previously, more details emerged that 25 passengers had survived the crash. We were hopeful that we would find my mother and little sister Anna.

We headed over to the country of the crash and visited the local administrative centre where we were handed a list of casualties. The names of my mother and litle Anna was not present in the list. There were five people who could not be identified. This made us very anxious and scared.

I was asked to identify if my family was among the five people who could not be identified. This was a harrowing experience with my heart skipping a beat each time. I removed the veil covering the dead bodies.

I was relived as if a huge bolder had been lifted off my shoulders.

The search for my parents continued. We soon began to visit hospitals in search for my little sister and mother.

I saw my mother in a local hospital she had suffered serious head injuries and had been in the hospital for six months since the crash. I was informed that she had lost her memory and was unable to recall anything about herself or her family. The doctors advised me that my mother needs to be in the hospital for some more days to help her recuperate. I agreed to the doctor's suggestion.

The question that haunted our mind now was where little Anna was. Nothing was known about her in the hospital where my mother was admitted. We were informed that she was brought in to the hospital alone and they knew nothing about the child.

We then contacted the local administration and explained our woes. They took us to an orphanage, where we looked for little Anna. The caretaker of the orphanage asked us to provide a photograph of little Anna to help him identify her. We expressed our inability to produce a photograph. I however tried to provide a very accurate description of little Anna. The warden recalled that a childless couple had visited the orphanage a month ago for the purpose of adoption. The warden gave us the contact details of the couple and wished that we find the little girl at the earliest.

We visited the couple where we saw little Anna playing gleefully. I was ecstatic upon looking at the little one. We sat down over a cup of tea and explained the complete story to them. They said that they had adopted Anna from the orphanage a month ago and would not send her with us as we did not have any means of looking after a young child. It was a tough call but in the best interest of the child we decided that to Anna live in the couple's house for the time being.

I had found my mother and little Anna both were fine but we were not able to reunite as a family due to unfavourable circumstances. Will we ever be able to get back together a family was question still needed some answering.

CHAPTER 6
THE RETURN HOME

We returned back to our adopted homeland where we were greeted to some good news, the government had announced a programme to allow refugees to return back to their homeland. The Professor was also thrilled as he could return to his homeland I was sceptical as we were yet to find my father and brother without whom the family would not be complete and we could not return home.

The professor wanted to return home and reunite with his countrymen. He convinced me that it was best for me to return back to my homeland and look for my father and brother and also complete my education.

Returning back to my homeland would enable me to complete my education and also secure a suitable job which will allow me to sustain myself after a long and hard thought I resultantly agreed with the professor to return back

We returned back to our homeland. We set out repairing our house which was partially damaged by the shelling, we were able to restore our home to its previous grandeur.

One day when I was just ready to leave for college, I received a call from the police officer asking me to visit the station. I visited the station and the police officer explained to me the events that had occurred at the airport on the fateful night that my brother and father went missing

My Father and brother managed to escape the firing at the airport and exited through the back gate where they were kidnapped by unknown men who blindfolded them and took them to an unknown location where they were tortured for about a couple of weeks before being shot down.

This was heart breaking for me I demanded that the perpetrators of such a heinous crime be punished. The police officer assured me that they would do everything that they possibly could to ensure justice.

---

* * *

35

ADRENALINE RUSH

INTRODUCTION

As we all sat across the dining table for dinner, my brother Joe announced that he had found a new job at Berryville a city 1800 miles away and he would have to move out the house in a few days. Everyone was very happy for him that he had found a new job but at the same time we were a bit sad that he had to move out of the house. We were a family of 6 people Me, my younger brother and my elder brother who lived with my parents and grandfather Gordon. We stayed together for as long as I can remember. My dad was a tool technician who ran his own workshop in the city. My younger brother was still a student at college. I worked at a small company near my home. My elder brother was the most intelligent amongst us siblings, He had completed his masters degree program from an elite university and was working as a team lead in a reputed firm. He seemed to be happy at work, his decision to switch jobs came in as a surprise for all of us.

Mom and Dad were unhappy at first to let their eldest son move to another city, they suggested that he find a job closer to home so that our family could stay together like before. Joe however was very keen on moving in to the new city as he felt that the job was more challenging and could bring out the best in him.

Mom and Dad tried their best to convince Joe that he should stay home and look for a job closer to home. There were a lot of arguments that took place between the three of them and that soured the relationships between them.

I and my little brother along with grandfather felt that something had to be done soon to prevent the relationship between Mom Dad and Joe further downhill. Grand Dad suggested that the 3 brothers along with Mom and Dad should go on a road trip in our customized home on wheels. He opined that travelling is the best way to create new bonds and to mend broken ones. I and my little brother were excited and asked Grand Dad to come along with us as well. He said that it is better he stays at home while we enjoy our trip. We reluctantly agreed.

The challenge that was now on our hands was to convince everybody to travel.

CHAPTER 2
THE CONVINCING

We set on our effort on convincing everyone about our plan to join us for the trip. It was by no means an easy effort to convince everyone. There was a lot of resistance to our efforts from both sides as no one wanted to travel with the other. Despite the resistance thanks to our persistent efforts and a bit of help from Grand-Dad we finally managed to convince everyone about our plan. My father agreed that he would come with us only because of me and my little brother and he also said that if there was ever a discussion about Joe's decision on the trip, He would return back home the very moment.

We were put in a tight spot as we had very little breathing space and a little word here and there would spoil the trip. I and Grand-Dad knew that we were taking a huge risk by getting everyone on board, but this was the only way that we could think of to get their relationships back on track. The next decision that was on our mind was the destination for our trip

This was likely to be a tricky choice as we had to choose a place which was suitable to everyone. The three of them did not seem to agree on anything the other one said or suggested the question that was on my mind was if we can find a location/destination that suits everyone
I and my little brother John with Grand-Dad Gordon sat down to think of a suitable place my little brother was of the opinion that we must visit an exotic location where we could enjoy our trip.

Grand-Dad said that such an idea was good but in the current situation where relationships between the father and son was not very good such a trip would not be enjoyable.

I had this thought in mind that this trip must be both enjoyable as well as heal the broken bonds between all the members. So, I suggested that we must try to recreate all the wonderful memories that we have had as a family.

It was a great idea exclaimed my grandfather who said that such a trip would not only be enjoyable but also heal the bonds that have been strained

It was trip down memory lane if you could call it that way

I managed to convince everyone with my plan and we were set for the journey. This journey would however be very different from any other one as we had to stay inside our customized vehicle for the entire duration of the trip.

CHAPTER 3
THE PREPARATION

My Dad got the vehicle repainted for the trip and all the minor repair works were carried out we all packed our bags and set out for an adventure All the essentials were packed up. We also had our bikes attached to the rear of the vehicle so that we could go cycling on the hills. Grandfather bid us an adieu and we set out on our journey.

CHAPTER 4
A BACKGROUND

We used to live at a place called Thomasville when we were young kids. It was a very quiet place with a very scenic environment. We used to live in a place that was surrounded by about 20 hectares of farmland where we used to grow wheat. It was a wonderful place to grow up amidst nature however we had all the amenities that were required for us to lead a happy life. Our school was located about a mile away from our home. There was a small ice-cream store which used to sell delightfully good strawberry ice-creams that were prepared right in front of our own eyes

Every place in that city had many stories associated with it. Will those old stories bring joy or sorrow is to be seen?

CHAPTER 5
THE UNEXPECTED HICCUP

We were all excited to commence our road trip at the break of dawn. When suddenly we heard a loud noise on the upper floors We ran across the stairway and we went into Mom's room where we found her moaning in pain. She had slipped and fallen on to the ground She was unable to get on her feet and had to be brought down to the lower floors by using a stretcher following which she was shifted to the hospital. X-Rays revealed that she had suffered a fracture in her left ankle her feet were soon plastered. She was advised not to place her feet on the floor for a couple of weeks.

We were now unsure as to what to do next as Mother was sick and father insisted that he would stay home to take care of Mother and Grandfather Gordon.

Joe and I had already taken leaves from our workplace for the trip. Dad advised us to go ahead as planned previously while he would stay home. We agreed reluctantly as we did not want to waste this opportunity to go on a trip.

Instead of our customized RV we decided to travel in our car as it was more comfortable for the three of us. We checked in all our bags and baggage's and were ready to leave home at the break of dawn

Due to the unexpected turn of events what began to be a family trip now became a brother's trip. Will the trip be the same keep reading to find out?

CHAPTER 6
THE PLAN CHANGES

Now that Mom and Dad were not around we siblings tried to change our plans a little bit. We headed straight towards the port city of Sutherville about 5 hours away. The trip was likely to be a very wild one as everything was unplanned. As we headed towards Sutherville we booked our tickets on a ferry to take us towards the islands. As we reached Sutherville we headed towards the hotel room which we had booked. We locked ourselves up in our hotel rooms for the next couple of hours. We then headed towards the harbor where we had a ferry ride booked.

We boarded the ferry it was a festive atmosphere everyone who was onboard seemed to enjoy his ride there was music singing and dancing. The view of the sunset was spectacular. We were all served dinner. We were to reach our destination at dawn.

It was very late at night as I was enjoying the cool sea breeze that was blowing across my face I was a few men who were struggling for their lives in the high seas. I immediately alerted the crew who threw the lifesaving equipment at them they held on to the lifesaving tubes the crew slowly rescued them and brought them on board. They were administered first aid and later provided food and water.

They carried a couple of bags one slung across their should and one tied to their waist. They wore tardy clothes and seemed exhausted. They were moved one of the vacant cabins and asked to rest.

I soon went to my room where I decided to put my head on the pillow and have a good night's rest. All the travelling had tired me and fell asleep as soon as I closed my eyelids.

I woke up the next morning and looked out of the cabin window to find all the crew and a few passengers who were on their knees. I did not understand what was happening but did sense that something was not right as when I looked at the clock it was 9 in the morning we had to reach our destination about a couple of hours earlier.

I soon reached out to my phone to call Joe and my younger brother to let them know about what I had seen but I could not place the call due to network troubles

I feared to move out of my cabin as I felt that I could be taken hostage just like the crew and the fellow passengers. I was unaware of my brother's whereabouts. I worried about their safety. Joe always had a satellite phone in his bag. But there was no way for me to contact him so I decided to stop worrying and step out of my cabin.

As I headed towards the door I heard a thud from the next cabin. There was loud screaming I was very scared and decided against moving out of my cabin. And hid under the bed I tried to lay completely still. My heart was pounding away.

As I lay under the bed I heard someone knocking on the door, I could not muster enough courage to open the door after some time the knocking stopped I was relived but I was still anxious about my brother's whereabouts I tried to reach out to them but was unsuccessful due to the lack of connectivity. I then realized that there was a telephone attached to one of the walls of my room. There was an emergency contact number inscribed on the name plate that was stuck close to the telephone

I soon got up and started dialing the emergency number that was displayed but unfortunately all the lines were busy and the call could not be completed.

I was scarred for the safety of my brother's and my own personal safety. Just as I lay on the floor thinking about my next move I began to hear noises of people moving down the stairs. I then peeped out of my cabin to find people being forced to de board at gun point. The ferry had come to a halt.

I waited for a while and then decided to follow those men. I slowly climbed down the stairway and followed the last gunman. I had to be very careful as any noise would be a giveaway and my life would be at stake. The men seemed to be taking all the passengers to an island. The island was full of thick trees and light was scarce It was a dense jungle. After walking for about twenty minutes all the passengers were taken to a cave that was dimly lit and I had to hide behind the trees as the entrance to the cave was well guarded.

As all the passengers entered the cave I hid behind the trees waiting for an opportunity to enter the cave. As I waited behind the thick canopy of trees the weather started to get rough and soon there were thick dark clouds which hovered over the trees a thunderstorm was eminent. The fear of a lightning strike was also very high the guards sensed danger and they quickly rushed into the cave for protection.

I grabbed this opportunity and tried to enter the cave as I neared the mouth of the cave visibility dropped and I could not see a thing in front of my eyes it was pitch dark.
I had no other choice but to go into the cave in order to rescue my brothers and the other passengers. I took the gamble and decided to go in.

I stepped into the cave I could sense that the floor underneath my feet was slushy and slippery but as I kept moving forward I could see a faint ray of light from a distance. I continued to move forward I heard the sound of water flowing it might have been a small stream which was flowing. I had to follow the sound of the stream as the visibility was still bare minimum. I kept following the sound of the stream and after walking for about 20 minutes I found a source of light emerging from the other end I realized that I may have found the other end of the cave.

There was no sight of the other passengers and my brothers I decided to go back and look for them I turned back and went along the same direction from where I had come from and soon after about 10 minutes the visibility was pitch dark but I could hear some noises. I decided to follow the noise as this could lead me to the place where the passengers were held captive.

Soon I saw bright light emanating, I decided to move forward in the direction of the light I soon found more armed men who were moving around the place with lanterns in their hands. I somehow managed to stay out of their sight and sneaked into the place where people were held captive.

I hid behind one of the rocks as I watched all the people being forced to kneel on their knees but what was to follow was beyond imagination.

CHAPTER 7
THE HOSTAGE PLAN

I saw my elder brother holding a gun and being instructed by who appeared to be the leader of the armed men to start killing the passengers one by one. Besides the leader was who appeared to be the leader's daughter but I recalled to her being someone familiar. I soon recalled that I had seen the girl's photos on my brother's mobile phone. I was in a state of shock with all theories and thoughts gushing into my head.

I however decided to lay low and watch everything that was unfolding before my eyes. My brother seemed reluctant to follow the leader's instructions and looked to be under severe stress just as this was unfolding there was a roaring noise all the armed men rushed out of the cave this gave me a small window of opportunity to come out of hiding and confront my brother

I soon came out of my hiding place and walked towards my brother, he appeared shocked looking at me I soon confronted him. He asked me to run away if I had to save myself, he also told me to take my little brother along. I refused to budge and asked him to explain all of the things that were unfolding in front of my eyes. He appeared to look away I held the gun barrel and pointed it towards my head and asked him to shoot me first before shooting anyone else as I could not bear the sight of my brother murdering innocent people. He soon broke into tears and went down on his knees and started apologizing for his actions He began to explain how he was trapped into this by the leader's daughter.

CHAPTER 8
THE TRAP

The leader's daughter and my brother were colleagues and were working in the same team on the same project. Everything seemed to be working fine until one day when the leader's daughter expressed her liking for my brother.

My brother at first was reluctant to agree but after persuasion agreed, they soon started sharing more time together both at work and outside work. One day my brother had given a set of confidential documents to the leader's daughter which were meant to be kept safely. The documents however were leaked by the leader's daughter, these documents could endanger public safety if they fell into the wrong hands. My brother soon confronted the lady and she replied that it was a mistake from her side and asked him to follow her instructions if no harm was to be caused to his reputation. It was a part of their plan to move my brother out of his house and make him quit his job. They intended to use my brother's intelligence for their unlawful activities. He also said that all the passengers aboard the ship were eminent scientists who were trapped as a part of the sinister plan to destroy a major tourist attraction. But it was very hard for me to know as to why he brought us along if he knew of the whole plan. I asked him why he brought us along with him? He said that he was tried everything that he possibly could to avoid this trip but could not. I empathized with him and said that we need to escape from here as soon as possible. He also agreed.

CHAPTER 9
THE ESCAPE

We soon untied all the passengers and moved out of the inner cave and were soon near the stream and I said that I knew a place from where I could escape and led them to the other end of the cave. There was a source of light emanating from the other end. We soon moved out one by one but soon we began to hear commotion from inside the cave the armed men may have had figured out our escape we soon decided to block the exit with rocks. The roaring noise that we had heard from inside the cave was due to a landslide that had taken place in the mountain above the landslide had blocked the entrance of the cave we soon closed the exit of the cave.

We now had to figure out how to get out of the island. We were able to see a beautiful beach in a distance we headed towards the sea hoping that we could find some ship or boat or try and contact someone to seek assistance. We soon were able to make contact with the emergency services and explained the situation. They soon dispatched a cargo ship which was sailing in the area. We were soon back to the port where we de-boarded and headed home.

My brother had to face an enquiry but his name was soon cleared from the case. The company also asked him to rejoin them. This trip which was meant to bridge broken bonds turned out be an unforgettable adventure

My brother soon realized the importance of having a family and apologized for his actions and decided to stay with us. We were all back as happy family
Until next time Goodbye

* * *

THE FINALE
AN UNEXPECTED TWIST

It is a hot summer day in the remote island town of Pasiese, Passise was a small dwelling of close to about 3000 people with fishing and movement of cargo being one the economic activities in this island.

The glaciers from the snow-capped mountain peak was the only source of fresh water to this island. This year however the situation was different a dry winter meant that there was very little snow. This worried the islanders who feared that their water source would dry up someday.

The islands decided that something had to be done before their only source of fresh water dries up. They decided to meet Dr Thompson who was a researcher at the prestigious Bluhahu Research Centre about 1000 miles from Passise.

The islanders met Dr Thompson who opined that this was a global phenomenon and further research has to be undertaken in order to understand the phenomenon and reverse its effects.

He assured the islanders that he would place a proposal in front of the President of the research centre for the allotment of funds for the project

Later that evening Dr Thompson met the president at his office and discussed the problem that he was trying to solve and its potential benefits to the people the president expressed his willingness to fund the project, but said to Mr Thompson that he had to find his own men to conduct research as there was an acute staff shortage at the facility.

Dr Thompson agreed and thanked the president for his consideration. He soon conveyed to the islanders about the President's decision to fund the project but also said that they need to find people who are willing to conduct research.

The next day Dr Thompson remembered about a young man who had saved his life while he was on a holiday. He recalled about the young man expressing his willingness to work on projects relating to environment and its conservation

Dr Thompson soon dialed Joe's number and asked him if he could meet the professor at the research Centre. Joe agreed and both of them had a meet where the professor explained to him about the problem he was trying to solve and asked Joe if he would be a part of this mission.

Joe readily agreed to the professor's request and asked if he could bring his brother's along too for helping him in his research. The professor agreed now Joe and his brothers were part of the research team

Dr Thompson conveyed to the residents of Pasiese about Joe and his brothers joining the professor in his research, the professor then instructs Joe and his brothers to head to a country which was ravaged by years of war in order to study about effects of the use of weapon systems on the environment.

Joe and his brothers then set out on their mission. They soon reach the capital of the war-ravaged country. The people of this nation were rebuilding their lives after many years of fighting. The scars of war were yet to heal. As Joe and his brothers reached the capital they receive a call from Professor Thompson informing them that they would stay at one his co-workers house while they conduct their research.

He also went on to say that he would personally receive them at the airport. Soon Joe and his brothers underwent through all the security checks and were soon at the arrival terminal.

They soon saw a young man holding a place card with "Joe" written on it Joe went straight up to him and shook his hands and introduced himself and his brothers. The young man introduced himself and soon they all went to the professor's home.

The professor greeted them and they sat down over a cup of tea. The professor recalled his association with Thompson. He shared many stories of their days together conducting research. The professor soon introduced his family to Joe and his brothers.

Joe asked the professor about the boy who had received them at the airport. The professor replied that he was John, one of his students who had lost his family in the war, and was currently staying with him.

Joe met John and heard his heart wrenching tale of how war separated him from his mother and little sister Anna. He recalled that he was unable to get back together with his family even though he knew where they lived.

Joe asked John if he would be interested in joining their research. John replied affirmatively, and said that it would be great honor to help them in their research.

Joe informed Thompson about a new member joining their efforts. As they set about to conduct their research. John took Joe and his brothers to his native village where they lived before the war began.

In what was now empty land once lived a very happy family he recalled. He also explained about the kind of weapons that were used during the war. They also visited the local hospital where they interviewed doctors and nurses asking them about the use of chemical weapons. They found that chemical weapons were used during the war. They also met locals who said that it was now harder for them to grow crops due to the soil becoming barren due to the of the chemical weapons. They also noticed vegetation dying down in the area, they soon collected all the relevant samples and flew back to professor Thompson and reported their findings.

Professor Thompson thanked the boys for their help and said that recent satellite imagery may indicate that the effects of climate change needs to be reversed quickly or we could move to point of no return.

Professor Thompson said that there were two small islands both in the opposite sides of the planet. In these islands there were reports of extremely rare mineral resource existing which could hold the key to reversing the effects of climate change.

He warned the boys that little is known about the island's inhabitants or vegetation and entire mission needs to be extremely secretive as any leaks could lead to prosecution.

The group was split into 2 teams one comprised of Joe and his younger brother they headed towards islands in the north. Joe's elder brother and John headed towards the islands in the south

John and Joe set of to the islands by sea, it was a dangerous journey because of the rough sea. The islands were usually battered by very heavy rain and the region experienced cyclonic storms almost throughout the year.

Both of them got down at the nearest harbor which was about 6 hours away from the islands, they decided to stay in the city for the night and begin their journey at the break of dawn.

Both the men were looking for a place to stay put for the night. They then saw an old building with a tattered signboard which said "Rooms for rent" both of them went in and saw an old lady at the reception desk. She was pale and lean with wrinkles all over her face, she was busy knitting a sweater. The men approached the old lady and said that they were looking for a room for a night's stay.

The old lady looked up to them and said "Nice to see some young men visit us after a long time" She also said that the rent would be 15$ per night and she added that dinner would be served in their rooms, she gave the young men a register and asked them to write all their details.

The two men went in and freshened up it was about 19:45 in the evening, The two men called Professor Thompson and told them that they had reached the harbor safely and had decided to begin their journey towards the islands at the break of dawn. The Professor wished them luck and advised them to exercise caution and stay safe.

Just as Joe ended the call the two of them heard the knocking of their door, they opened the door to see that the old lady had bought them dinner, it was a sumptuous 3 course meal. She served dinner to the guests and sat down on a chair. Joe then asked the old lady if she was the only person who was looking after the place as they could find no one around

The old Lady said that this place was their home for many decades, the old lady lived with her husband and daughter, Joe then asked the lady about her husband and daughter. The old lady replied with a sober tone and a tear in her eye that her husband was an explorer and miner by profession, many years ago he heard that there was a plethora of gold waiting to be found at some island near the coast. He set out on an expedition with a few men but little was heard of him afterwards said the old lady as she wiped her tears.

Joe and John grew more curious and wondered if it was the same islands they were heading towards. They then told the old lady about their expedition; the old lady grew anxious and asked the two boys to abandon their mission as the place was too dangerous.

She said that there was folklore about the islands being inhabited by many dangerous snakes and wild beasts which would kill anyone who managed to enter the islands. She also added that none of the people who had tried to explore the islands had returned back alive, but the young men told the lady about the importance of their mission and how they were trying to reverse the effects of climate change. The old lady reluctantly agreed as both of them completed their meals, The boys then thanked the old for all the hospitality and decided to call it a day.

The next morning both the men woke up and got ready for their mission, the old woman wished them luck and handed them an old hunting rifle for their safety and wished them luck.

The men headed towards the harbor where they had a ferry waiting for them. The two men boarded the ferry and Joe steered it towards the islands as John kept a watch. After about 6 hours of travel they finally reached their destination. Thy anchored their ferry and got down, They started walking away from the coast. The islands were beautiful with many kinds of flowering plants and huge trees which gave them a lot of shade.

The two men kept walking inward they saw that the vegetation was getting thicker as they moved. It was getting darker and darker with as the day progressed. The men kept walking however to their surprise there was no sign of any wild beasts as indicated by the old lady. The men soon reached the middle of a forest it was a beautiful place there was a waterfall due to a stream flowing from the top of a mountain ridge.

There was a cave at the base of the mountain. The two men decided to enter the cave, they entered the cave it was dark and scary but the 2 men decided to continue their journey with the help of torches They soon discovered that these caves had carvings of people engraved on them. They seem to be depicting pictures of a great civilization that existed a long time ago. These pictures were as though they depicted a story. As the men went in there were pictures of men being beaten up and chained all of these people seemed to be holding shovels in their hands. It became clear that there was some mineral wealth around this place. As they progressed further the depictions began to disappear. The two men were really tired but kept moving as they felt that it would be unsafe to stay inside the cave as it was dark.

They soon started to hear some noise and felt that they were close to the end of the tunnel. They moved closer as their legs ached and backs moaned in pain. After walking for about an hour they finally saw the light of the moon that was beaming through one of the tunnels they felt that they had reached the other end.
They soon went out of those caves it was dark as the moonlight shined upon them. They walked further and decided to rest under a tree, and continue their journey the next day.

They were soon woken up by the noise of people walking/marching. They decided to stay awake and followed the noise this was when they found many tents with people living in them. These people were holding guns and standing guard. The two men decided to sneak in amidst the darkness. They soon went inside a compound which was surrounded by many guards. The men soon discovered that there was mine field where some mineral was being mined they decided to hide behind one of those tents and keep a watch on the activities. The next morning the two men woke up and were surprised to see the other 2 guys who had left for the islands in the south being in the same place. They then saw a chopper land on one of the lands marked H John and Joe were shocked to see Professor Thompson getting down from one of them.

It was all confusion as to why would the professor send us on such an arduous journey if he could reach the place by a chopper. And why would he lie to them that he knew nothing of this place. John and Joe then decide to keep a tab on the professor's activities. It is then noticed that the mineral was loaded on to ships and being ferried to various places of the world. Everything seemed hazy until Joe and John were caught by the guards and they took him to the professor. The professor remarked "Oh I see that you boys have made it" I thought you wouldn't be able to bear this arduous journey and would die midway. The boys were still confused as to why the professor would lie to them. Then a man emerged from behind the professor. He was tall well-built and wore glasses. Instantly John remarked "He is my father". Everyone was gazing at each other's faces. It was then when professor Thompson started speaking "Confused aren't you, You are right he is your father he is helping me in my quest to become the most powerful man in the world he remarked" Professor Thompson said that he had a young son who had who had committed suicide by jumping off the roof of his house because he couldn't get a job in the company he hoped for" Just then Joe's brother said that he had a friend in college who did a similar thing.". This was when Thompson replied that you are right the friend you were referring to was my son, He was brilliant and always wanted to be at the top" but you ruined his chance, but Joe's brother was aghast saying that he was one of his closest friends and meant him no harm at all.

The professor then continued saying that he was the mastermind behind the kidnapping of Joe and his brother's but unfortunately could not kill them.

John then asked what his dad was doing here while he was searching for his mother and sister in an unknown country. John's father then revealed that their house was bombed during the war not by the opponent's but the president's own forces as he was secretly trying to topple the government and he was the reason the civil war started. John was shocked and asked why he did this and what happened to Anna and Mommy on that day. John's father revealed that his elder brother was killed in a gunfight with the security forces while he managed to escape from the airport, he stated that he knew little about Anna and her mother. He said that joined Thompson's hand in his quest to become the president of the country and rule over the land. John was shocked.

But a question still remained what was the mineral the professor was transporting and why was it a secret. They asked the professor about this he replied stating that these are not minerals that are used to treat global warming but are rare metals that are found only in these islands, these minerals are used to make shields and jackets that protect us from radioactive emissions in the case of a nuclear bombing. And several minerals are found in the other islands which is connected to this via a deep-sea tunnel (South islands) which can be used to make the most destructive and dangerous weapons in the world.

The men were shocked to hear about the professor's intentions but there was no way to stop him as they were surrounded by hundreds of guards who pledged alliance to the professor.

Just then military aircrafts began to buzz above their heads everyone was surprised as this was a place that was known only to a few people. Professor Thompson was tried to escape but his chopper was immobilized by gunfire but a gun fight ensued. The Professor and his men had to surrender and admit defeat.

A question still lingered in everyone's mind about who informed the military. This was when one of the men got down from a military helicopter. John instantly seemed to recognize him, he was none other than Anna's adopted father. He explained to John that his mother had regained her memory and explained to them about your dad's dubious intentions that was when I escalated the matter to our Hon President who opined that urgent action must be taken to prevent any further harm to innocent people. John's father and the professor were arrested and sentenced to death for treachery and war crimes.

John returned back to his mother and sister Joe and his brothers lived happily at their home, the puzzling question was about did how Anna's adopted father come to know about us visiting the island's. Was the old lady in the hotel a spy who was tracking us, Well she is the only one who probably knows the answer, but that may never be revealed..

We ultimately have many options which we can exercise to make the situation better or worse for us and for others as well. Human mind always reacts to various situations in different ways

For one it may be about himself first and others later but for someone else it may be about other's first and himself later. Some people may be looking for a reason to live while others live for a particular reason.

It is ultimately our choices which define the kind of life we lead. Choices which may seem impossible at the start may lead to amazing things we never expected. A choice can lead you on a path to heaven or hell Choose wisely

* * *